Sounds All Around Us

Making Sounds

Charlotte Guillain

www.heinemannlibrary.co.uk
Visit our website to find out more
information about Heinemann
Library books.

To order:

☎ Phone +44 (0) 1865 888066

📄 Fax +44 (0) 1865 314091

💻 Visit www.heinemannlibrary.co.uk

Heinemann is an imprint of Capstone Global Library Limited, a
company incorporated in England and Wales having its registered
office at 7 Pilgrim Street, London, EC4V 6LB – Registered company
number: 6695582

"Heinemann" is a registered trademark of Pearson Education
Limited, under licence to Capstone Global Library Limited

Edited by Charlotte Guillain, Rebecca Rissman, and
Catherine Veitch
Designed by Joanna Hinton-Malivoire
Picture research by Tracy Cummins and Tracey Engel
Originated by Heinemann Library
Printed by South China Printing Company Limited

ISBN 978 0 431 19336 6 (hardback)
13 12 11 10 09
10 9 8 7 6 5 4 3 2 1

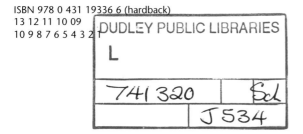
British Library Cataloguing in Publication Data
Guillain, Charlotte
Making sounds. - (Sounds all around us)
534
A full catalogue record for this book is available from the
British Library.

Acknowledgements
The author and publishers are grateful to the following for
permission to reproduce copyright material: Alamy pp. **4
top left** (©UpperCut Images), 5 (©Digital Vision), **9**
(©Images of Africa Photobank); ageFotostock pp. **18**
(©Creatas), **23a** (©Creatas); CORBIS pp. **11** (©TempSpor/
Dimitri Iundtt), **23c** (©TempSpor/Dimitri Iundtt); Getty
Images pp. **6** (©Red Chopsticks), **7** (©Bernd Opitz), **10** (©Mike
Harrington), **12** (©Ariel Skelley), **16** (©Matthieu Ricard), **19**
(©Adam Gault), **23b** (©Adam Gault); PhotoEdit Inc. p. **20**;
Photolibrary pp. **13** (©Digital Vision), **14** (©Tim Pannell), **15**
(©Blend Images RF/Terry Vine/Patrick Lane), **21** (©Digital
Vision/Jeffrey Coolidge Photography), iStockphoto pp. **4 top
right** (©Frank Leung), **4 bottom right** (©Peter Viisimaa);
Shutterstock pp. **4 bottom left** (©devi), **8** (©Sonya Etchison),
17 (©Leah-Anne Thompson).

Cover photograph of Stomp Out Loud cast members reproduced
with permission of Landov (©Reuters/Las Vegas Sun/Steve
Marcus). Back cover photograph of a girl kicking leaves
reproduced with permission of Getty Images (©Mike Harrington).

The publishers would like to thank Nancy Harris and Adriana
Scalise for their assistance in the preparation of this book.

Every effort has been made to contact copyright holders of
any material reproduced in this book. Any omissions will
be rectified in subsequent printings if notice is given to
the publisher.

Contents

Sounds

There are many different sounds.

We hear different sounds around us every day.

Sounds our bodies make

We can make many different sounds.

We can use our bodies to
make sounds.

We can use our hands to
make sounds.

We can clap our hands.

We can use our feet to make sounds.

We can stamp our feet.

We can use our voices to
make sounds.

We can use our voices to sing.

We can use our voices to shout.

We can use our voices to whisper.

We can use our mouths to
make sounds.

We can use our mouths to whistle.

Other sounds we can make

We can bang things to make sounds.

We can scrape things to make sounds.

We can shake things to make sounds.

We can press things to make sounds.

What have you learned?

- We can use our hands to make sounds.

- We can use our feet to make sounds.

- We can use our mouths and voices to make sounds.

- We can make sounds using many other things.

Picture glossary

 **bang** sudden loud noise

 **scrape** rub against something hard or rough

 **stamp** bring your foot down firmly on the ground

Index

Note to parents and teachers
Before reading
Tell the children that there are sounds all around us every day. Explain that there are different ways we can make sounds using our bodies and other things. Ask the children to discuss ways of making different sounds and to make a list of their ideas.

After reading
• Look back at the list with the children. Ask volunteers to circle sounds that were in the book. Then have a few of the children make that sound with their bodies or things in the classroom.
• Pass around musical instruments and ask the children to make their own sounds. Instruct them to play their instruments loudly and quietly. Ask them what they had to do to make loud and quiet sounds.